JAPANESE MYTHOLOGY

Amaterasu

BY GOLRIZ GOLKAR

CONTENT CONSULTANT
MATTHIEU FELT, PhD
ASSISTANT PROFESSOR OF JAPANESE
UNIVERSITY OF FLORIDA

Kids Core
An Imprint of Abdo Publishing
abdobooks.com

abdobooks.com

Published by Abdo Publishing, a division of ABDO, PO Box 398166, Minneapolis, Minnesota 55439.

Printed in the United States of America, North Mankato, Minnesota.
102024
012025

THIS BOOK CONTAINS RECYCLED MATERIALS

Cover Photo: Shutterstock Images
Interior Photos: Shutterstock Images, 4–5, 7, 12, 16, 24, 28 (top); John Stevenson/Asian Art & Archaeology, Inc./Corbis Historical/Getty Images, 8; Red Line Editorial, 10; Kawanabe Kyosai/The Connoisseur, 14–15; History and Art Collection/Alamy, 18; The Asahi Shimbun/Getty Images, 20–21, 29 (bottom); Sean Pavone/Shutterstock Images, 22, 29 (top); POL/BT/Alamy, 25 , 28 (bottom); Everett Kennedy Brown/EPA/Shutterstock Images, 26

Editor: Christa Kelly
Series Designer: Ryan Gale

Library of Congress Control Number: 2024938390

Publisher's Cataloging-in-Publication Data

Names: Golkar, Golriz, author.
Title: Amaterasu / by Golriz Golkar
Description: Minneapolis, Minnesota: ABDO Publishing, 2025 | Series: Japanese mythology | Includes online resources and index.
Identifiers: ISBN 9781098295936 (lib. bdg.) | ISBN 9798384916932 (ebook)
Subjects: LCSH: Mythology, Japanese--Juvenile literature. | Deities--Juvenile literature. | Amaterasu (Shinto deity)--Juvenile literature. | Great Divinity Illuminating Heaven (Shinto deity)--Juvenile literature. | Mythology, Asian--Juvenile literature.
Classification: DDC 398.21--dc23

CONTENTS

Amaterasu's name translates to "Great Goddess Lighting Up Heaven."

CHAPTER 1

A Land of Darkness

An ancient Japanese story tells of a time when the sun did not shine. Both Earth and the heavens went dark. Without sunlight, rice could not grow. Evil spirits took over, bringing chaos. Gods and goddesses cried and moaned. They were sad and frightened.

The world was missing the light of Amaterasu (pronounced ah-mah-teh-rah-soo), the Japanese sun goddess.

It all began with a visit from Amaterasu's brother Susanoo (soo-sah-no-oh). He was the storm god. He destroyed her home. He ruined the rice fields her light shined upon. Amaterasu became scared and angry. She shut herself inside a cave. She vowed never to come out.

The gods and goddesses knew they needed to bring back Amaterasu. They came up with a plan. They put a rooster outside her cave. They also put a tree outside the cave entrance. It was covered in jewels and beautiful pieces of cloth. Finally, the gods hung a mirror from the tree.

The Shinto god of wisdom, Omoikane, came up with a plan to get Amaterasu out of the cave.

Today, the Amano Iwato cave where Amaterasu hid is considered holy.

The rooster crowed. Amaterasu was startled. Did that mean there had been a sunrise? She listened carefully. She heard singing and laughing. The other gods called out to Amaterasu. They told her that a more beautiful goddess had taken her place. She was no longer needed.

Amaterasu was confused. Who could be more beautiful than her? She opened the cave door. She peeked outside.

Amaterasu saw her reflection in the mirror. She was dazzled by her beauty. With Amaterasu distracted, the other gods and goddesses pulled her outside. Amaterasu's light swept away the darkness, and the Earth and the heavens lit up again.

Where in the World Is Japan?

More than 125 million people live in Japan.

What Is Japanese Mythology?

Japan is an island country. It lies off the eastern coast of Asia. Hundreds of years ago, people in Japan began writing stories called myths. Japanese myths are often about gods and heroes. Other myths explain why natural events happen.

Shinto and Kami

The Shinto religion honors *kami*, or "spirits." Gods and goddesses are kami. So are some monsters. Kami are also found in nature. Rocks, waterfalls, plants, and animals can be kami. People who have passed away can be kami too.

People have worshiped Amaterasu for more than 1,000 years.

Japanese myths are part of the Shinto religion. *Shinto* means "way of the gods." Nearly 89 million people in Japan practice Shinto.

Some of the most famous Japanese myths are about Amaterasu. Many consider her to be Japan's most important god. Hundreds of years after her story was first told, Amaterasu still plays an important role in Japanese culture.

Explore Online

Visit the website below. Does it give any new information about Shinto that wasn't in Chapter One?

Shinto

abdocorelibrary.com/amaterasu

Izanami and Izanagi, *right*, had hundreds of children, including Amaterasu, *left*.

CHAPTER 2

The Sun Goddess

Amaterasu is the daughter of the god Izanagi. He and the goddess Izanami created Japan. One day, Izanagi visited the underworld. When he came back, he went to a river to clean himself. As he washed his left eye, Amaterasu was born.

Amaterasu was loved by both gods and humans. She helped humans start farming.

When he washed his right eye, the moon god Tsukuyomi (soo-koo-yo-mee) was born. Washing his nose gave birth to Susanoo.

Izanagi gave Amaterasu a jeweled necklace. He told her to rule the heavens. She listened to her father and ruled well.

Amaterasu was beautiful. She gave light to all creatures. She was kind to the other gods and goddesses. She was also mighty. After leaving her cave, Amaterasu showed her power. She and the other gods cast Susanoo out of heaven. Amaterasu then decided to bring Japan under her **descendants'** rule.

Susanoo's Challenge

One day, Susanoo challenged Amaterasu to a contest. He wanted to see who could have the most sons. Susanoo gave Amaterasu his sword. She used it to make three girls. She gave Susanoo her jewels. He used it to make five boys. Because the boys were created from her jewels, Amaterasu decided that she was the winner of the contest.

Legend says the world was in chaos before Amaterasu, *top left*, sent Ninigi, *top middle*, to rule the land.

Ruling Japan

Amaterasu called for her grandson Ninigi (nee-nee-gee). She told him that he would rule Earth. Before he was sent to Japan, she gave him three **sacred** treasures. One was a sword. The second was a jewel that had hung on the tree by her cave. The last was the mirror that the gods had used to distract her.

Armed with Amaterasu's gifts, Ninigi looked important. He went to see the powerful god Okuninushi (oh-koo-nee-noo-shee), the ruler of Japan. Ninigi convinced the god to let him be the new ruler. Ninigi's great-grandson Jimmu went on to become the first **emperor** of Japan.

Further Evidence

Look at the website below. Does it give any new evidence to support Chapter Two?

Ninigi

abdocorelibrary.com/amaterasu

In 2019, Naruhito, *left*, became the emperor of Japan.

CHAPTER 3

Honoring Amaterasu

Modern Japan is led by an **imperial** family. The family traces its **lineage** back to Amaterasu. The imperial family still keeps the sun goddess's sword, jewel, and mirror today. Only emperors and Shinto priests are allowed to look at the items.

Ise Grand Shrine is made up of 125 smaller shrines.

The treasures are used during the ceremony to crown each new emperor.

Japan honors Amaterasu with various **shrines**. The most important shrine in Japan is the Ise Grand Shrine. It is about 2,000 years old. It is dedicated to Amaterasu. Shinto followers perform about 1,500 **rituals** there every year. They pray for a good harvest, world peace, and happiness for the imperial family. People from all over the world visit the shrine each year.

Rebuilding the Shrine

The Ise Grand Shrine was created 1,000 years ago. It is rebuilt every 20 years. Rebuilding the shrine preserves the original design. This tradition also brings the community together. Locals help rebuild the shrine. Old materials are then used to build other shrines.

Statues throughout Japan celebrate Amaterasu.

Amaterasu in Art

Amaterasu is often shown in Japanese art. She usually has long hair and colorful clothing. Sunbeams shine around her, showing that she is the sun goddess.

The sun goddess is celebrated in Japanese prints. People carve her image on blocks of wood. The blocks are then covered in ink. Paper is pressed onto the blocks to make prints.

Utagawa Toyokuni was a printmaker. Several of his prints depict the cave myth.

Many artworks depict the cave myth. The goddess is shown opening the cave door. Gods and goddesses are nearby. A rooster, mirror, and tree are often found in these images.

Amaterasu is honored during many Japanese celebrations, including the Kannamesai festival.

Modern artists also celebrate Amaterasu. The sun goddess is often found in manga. These are Japanese comic books. She is also found in Japanese cartoons called anime. Some video games also feature Amaterasu as a character. Hundreds of years after her story was first told, Amaterasu remains a beloved Japanese goddess.

Primary Source

Helen Hardacre studies Japanese religions. She explains the importance of shrines:

> Wherever new settlements are founded, a shrine . . . would be [built] for the spirits of that place, as a way of honoring them and [asking for] their [kindness] and protection. . . . Without a shrine, a place is "unfit for human **habitation**," because proper relations with the kami have not been established.

Source: Helen Hardacre. *Shinto: A History*. Oxford University, 2017, p. 1.

What's the Big Idea?

Read the quote. What is its main idea? Explain how the main idea is supported by details.

Legendary Facts

Amaterasu is the Japanese sun goddess.

When Amaterasu shut herself inside a cave, the Earth and heavens went dark. Other gods and goddesses tricked her to bring her back.

Many Japanese shrines honor Amaterasu.

The modern imperial family is said to be descended from Amaterasu.

Glossary

descendants
people who are related to a person who lived in the past

emperor
the ruler of an empire

habitation
the state of living in a particular place

imperial
relating to an emperor or empire

lineage
a line of ancestry, or the people in one's family

rituals
actions carried out in a specific way, often related to a religious ceremony

sacred
describing something important, often with religious value

shrine
a place where gods and other religious figures are honored and worshipped

Online Resources

To learn more about Amaterasu and Japanese mythology, visit our free resource websites below.

Core Library CONNECTION
FREE! COMMON CORE MULTIMEDIA RESOURCES

Visit **abdocorelibrary.com** or scan this QR code for free Common Core resources for teachers and students, including vetted activities, multimedia, and booklinks, for deeper subject comprehension.

Booklinks NONFICTION NETWORK
FREE! ONLINE NONFICTION RESOURCES

Visit **abdobooklinks.com** or scan this QR code for free additional online weblinks for further learning. These links are routinely monitored and updated to provide the most current information available.

Learn More

Hudak, Heather C. *Susanoo*. Abdo, 2025.

Kaiser, Emma. *Tsukuyomi*. Abdo, 2025.

Yasuda, Yuri. *Japanese Myths, Legends, and Folktales: Bilingual English and Japanese Edition*. Tuttle, 2019.

Index

About the Author

Golriz Golkar has written more than 100 nonfiction and fiction books for children. She holds a BA in American literature and culture from UCLA and an EdM in language and literacy from the Harvard Graduate School of Education. She loves to write the kinds of books that students are excited to read.